P9-CKD-797

Free-Motion Quilting
with Angela Walters

*Choose & Use Quilting Designs
for Modern Quilts*

stashBOOKS®
an imprint of C&T Publishing

Text copyright © 2012 by Angela Walters

Photography and Artwork copyright © 2012 by C&T Publishing, Inc.

Publisher: Amy Marson

Creative Director: Gailen Runge

Art Director: Kristy Zacharias

Editor: Liz Aneloski

Technical Editors: Sadhana Wray
and Ann Haley

Cover/Book Designer: April Mostek

Production Coordinator: Jessica Jenkins

Production Editor: S. Michele Fry

Illustrator: Aliza Shalit

Photography by Christina Carty-Francis and Diane Pedersen of C&T Publishing, Inc.,
unless otherwise noted

Cover photography by Briana Gray (Shades of Gray Photography)

Published by Stash Books, an imprint of C&T Publishing, Inc., P.O. Box 1456,
Lafayette, CA 94549

Library of Congress Cataloging-in-Publication Data

Walters, Angela, 1979-

Free-motion quilting with Angela Walters : choose & use quilting designs
on modern quilts / Angela Walters.

    p. cm.

ISBN 978-1-60705-535-8 (soft cover)

1. Quilting--Design. 1. Title.

TT835.W35653 2012

746.46--dc23

                    2011043262

Printed in China

10 9 8 7

Dedication

This one's for you, Grandpa Ford.

Thank you for investing time into my life. You taught me much more than quilting. I learned that family comes first and that ice cream sandwiches are a necessity. You were my biggest supporter, and I would not have found my passion for quilting if it weren't for you.

I pray that I am as patient with my grandchildren as you were with me.

I love and miss you.

Acknowledgments

Wow! Where do I start? It has been said that you know who your friends are when it's time to move. But I don't agree. You know who your friends are when you are knee-deep in book writing, stressed out, and not sure how it's all going to come together. More than a few people were there for me.

To my husband, Jeremy, for never letting me quit.

To C&T Publishing, Robert Kaufman Fabrics company, Quilters Dream Batting, and Superior Threads. Thanks for believing in me and my book.

To everyone who helped make this book possible, by helping piece quilts, giving me fabric, or letting me use their quilt patterns:

Alissa Haight Carlton	Heidi Hendrickson
Mark Cesarik	Jessica Levitt
Jenifer Dick	Georgieanna Martin (my awesome mom!)
Jacquie Gering	Modern Quilt Relish patterns
Scott Hansen	Tula Pink
Shea Henderson	Debi Walters (my awesome mother-in-law!)

And a special, heartfelt thank-you for a woman who took a chance on a brand-new quilter almost ten years ago—love you, Kathy!

CONTENTS

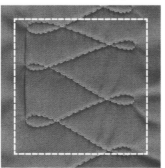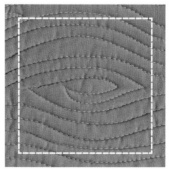

INTRODUCTION

Like a lot of other younger quilters, I didn't set out to be a quilter. Instead, quilting found me. Not long after I met my soon-to-be husband, he introduced me to his family. This included his Grandpa Ford, who loved to make quilts. At the time I wasn't even sure what a quilt was. Grandpa, as he immediately insisted I call him, quickly changed that.

After a year of admiring his many quilts, I asked him to show me how to make one. He was so patient with me, instructing me to carefully cut out nine squares with scissors and templates. I then began the process of sewing them into a Nine-Patch block. Proud of my creation, I showed it to him. He agreed that it looked great, and with a mischievous gleam in his eyes, he said, "Now let me show you the easy way!" He produced a rotary cutter and a mat, and so began my love of quilting.

One day, he suggested I buy a quilting machine. Never having seen a quilting machine, I wholeheartedly agreed. I called the Gammill company, and they happened to have a used one for sale. As quick as a blink, it was delivered and set up.

Up to that point, my Grandpa (at this point he was my Grandpa, too) had sent our quilts to a machine quilter who could quilt three patterns. Based on that, I assumed quilting machines could quilt only three patterns, and I was pretty sure they would quilt themselves. I quickly figured out that I had been incorrect, but by that time, I was head-over-heels in love with quilting.

I learned several free-motion quilting designs and started quilting for customers. I was perfectly happy quilting traditional quilts with traditional designs, and I would have continued along had I not been introduced to the modern quilting community.

On a whim, I attended the inaugural meeting of the Kansas City Modern Quilting Guild. During the first meeting, I was in awe of the quilts I saw. Bright and bold, full of graphic designs, they were unlike anything I had ever seen. Soon, I was asked to quilt some modern quilts. I very quickly realized they couldn't be approached in the same way as traditional quilts.

Traditional quilts are fairly predictable. They usually have a regular layout, often including sashing and borders. Modern quilts, on the other hand, offer irregular shapes, random placement, and bold fabrics. As I quilted more and more modern quilts, I realized I loved quilting—modern quilts especially. Quilting is the most fun part! I am writing this book to pass my love of quilting on to you. My hope is that you will love machine quilting as much as I do!

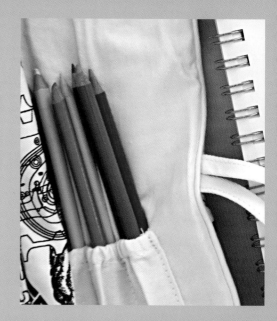

Section 1:
GETTING STARTED

I often tell anyone who will listen that the quilting is the most fun part of quiltmaking. Some quilters will agree with me, nodding with enthusiasm. But more often than not, quilters will roll their eyes and walk away, muttering under their breath. For a newer quilter, it can all be so overwhelming. Don't be discouraged! The first section of the book will help get you started. You will find out what this book is—and isn't—as well as what you need to get started. This includes not only the supplies but also the mind-set you will need to be successful.

So let go of your doubts and get ready to quilt—the modern way!

BEFORE
YOU START

The modern quilting community is alive and thriving—there is no denying it. If you go online and take a look at the many, many blogs featuring beautiful modern quilts, you can't help but be inspired. But over and over, I see quilters piecing such beautiful quilt tops only to resort to an allover quilting design, unsure of how to quilt it or doubtful about their quilting ability.

As a machine quilter, I see quilting as another layer of art, the very definition of form and function. The quilting should complement the quilt top and make it look the best it can be. I often say that quilting is like putting on makeup. Makeup artists don't put blush all over the face; instead they use different types of makeup in different areas of the face. In the same way, we should consider the quilt top when deciding on the quilting designs.

I will admit that some quilts need an allover design, but most quilts will benefit from custom quilting. This book will walk you through the process of learning the designs and how to use them on common modern quilts.

Also, the glossary of terms and phrases (page 118) may be useful as you go through this book on your modern machine quilting journey.

Before we start, let's discuss what this book is and isn't.

What This Book Is

This book is divided into three sections: Getting Started, The Designs, and Using the Designs in Modern Quilts. But these sections also could be described as Motivation, Instruction, and Inspiration: First, I want to motivate you to push your quilting boundaries and try new designs. Second, I will teach you several of my favorite designs. Last, I want to inspire you with pictures of common modern quilts and different ways to quilt them.

What This Book Isn't

This book isn't made up of hard-and-fast rules. What I teach are things that have worked for me. Just as in all areas of quilting, do what you like; do what you want to do.

This book isn't a longarm quilting book; it is a machine quilting book. Whether you use a longarm machine or a domestic sewing machine (DSM), these designs are for you.

What Exactly Is Modern Machine Quilting?

Quilting looks best when it complements the quilt top. So *modern machine quilting* could also be called *quilting modern quilts*. The quilting is modern because it is used on a modern quilt. This book will show several designs; some may be considered modern, and some may not. It isn't just the designs you use but also the way you use them, that makes the difference.

Learning the Designs

Draw, Draw, Draw

I love to say that 80 percent of quilting is knowing where to go next. (Surely there is a mathematical algorithm to prove this.) When asked how to get better at quilting, I always tell quilters to practice drawing the designs over and over on paper until they are comfortable with the design. Draw a box and fill it with the design you are practicing. By doing this, you will learn how to fill the space evenly and how not to get yourself stuck in a corner.

Don't Be Too Hard on Yourself

When your nose is two inches from the quilt top, you can see every little imperfection. Remember that every little mistake adds character, and you probably won't notice it from a few feet away. When you are finished with the quilt, put it away for a day. When you pull it out the next day, set it across the room and admire it from afar. Chances are, it will look great.

Remember! Practice Makes Perfect

Anything worth doing well takes a lot of practice. One common misconception is that some people instantly know how to machine quilt. But you can ask accomplished machine quilters and they will tell you that it takes a lot of time and practice. So don't get discouraged; keep practicing, and you will get the hang of it.

SUPPLIES

Below is a list of what you might need to get started.

Note: *The supplies and products I use are my favorites, but that doesn't mean others don't work as well. Experiment until you find what works best for you and your machine.*

The Machine: Longarm or Sewing Machine?

Don't be tricked into thinking you need a longarm quilting machine to machine quilt your own quilts. While it does make quilting easier, it definitely isn't a necessity. All the designs in this book can be quilted using a domestic sewing machine (DSM) or a longarm.

The same goes for all the available add-ons. For instance, I quilt on a Gammill longarm, but it is the smallest longarm available. It doesn't have a stitch regulator or a needle up-and-down function. All it has is a speed control and an on–off switch. And that is just fine for me!

Thread

My favorite thread is So Fine by Superior Threads.

If quilting is my therapy, then threads are my meds! I love to use many different thread colors. I am constantly asked what kind of thread I use. Because machine quilting is done at high speed, I use a thread made especially for machine quilting. I have used several different kinds of thread throughout the years, but I keep coming back to my all-time favorite—So Fine, by Superior. So Fine is a 50-weight polyester thread strong enough not to break but thin enough to blend.

I know, I know. Some of you are gasping out loud right now. I know it's not cotton thread, and some people use only cotton thread. I am not one of them. I like my quilting to blend into the quilt top, and cotton is much thicker than the So Fine I use, so it doesn't blend in as well. Cotton thread also produces too much lint, which clogs up my quilting machine.

Many different threads are on the market, so I encourage you to try several until you find what works for you.

What about Color?

When I pick out thread for a quilt, I usually choose one that matches the quilt top. Because I like a lot of quilting, a thread color that blends will add texture to the quilt without overpowering the quilt top. I believe the first thing people should see is the quilt top, and then, a split second later, they should see the quilting.

If a quilt is made up of several different colors, it can be hard to decide which color to use. Try laying several colors on the quilt top and see which one blends the most. I often use a light gray or light taupe thread on multicolor quilts.

Batting

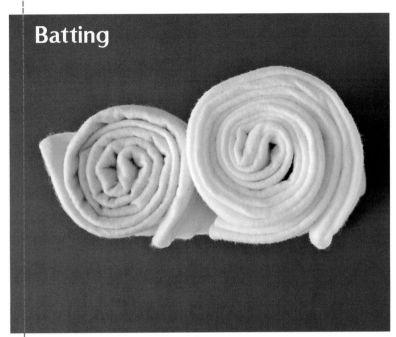

My favorite brand of batting is Quilters Dream.

The question I am asked most often is what batting I prefer, and my answer is always the same: Quilters Dream Batting. It has always been a favorite of mine. A bonus is that Quilters Dream is a family-owned business that sells only to quilt shops and quilting professionals.

It is a strong polyester batting, but it isn't too stiff. It is great for quilts that will need to hang or be displayed because it doesn't hold the fold lines as much as cotton batting.

Quilters Dream Cotton batting has a nice drape and softness. It is great for quilts that will be well-loved and cuddled under.

Other kinds of batting on the market include silk, bamboo, and poly-cotton blends to name a few. Experiment and see what you like the best.

Marking Tools

A variety of marking tools will make quilting easier.

Some people think that free-motion quilting means that you don't use markings of any kind. This is incorrect. Free-motion quilting refers to the fact that the quilting is hand guided. Using stencils and marking tools will help keep the designs consistent. It is my belief that every quilter, whether a longarmer or those using a DSM, should have an assortment of marking tools.

All of my quilting is free-motion, but sometimes I mark larger motifs on the quilt. I also use registration marks on my quilt. These marks help me ensure that designs are consistent. These are a few of my favorite marking tools:

Water-Soluble Pens

I will admit that I am a snob when it comes to water-soluble pens. I use only Dritz blue marking pens. I have never had a problem with the marks not coming out, so I figure, why try anything else? I am very cautious to remove the marks quickly, using only cold water, following the manufacturer's instructions.

Chalk

Chalk is a great way to mark dark fabrics or quilts that I don't want to get wet. Chalk pencils and chalk sticks are great for this purpose.

Stencils

Stencils are great for quickly marking designs on a quilt. The stencils I use most often are grids for marking registration lines. The registration lines help me keep my designs even. I use a chalk pounce pad to mark the stencils. The pad holds blue or white chalk and can be rubbed over the stencil to quickly mark the design. Stencils are available in all different shapes and sizes.

tip

When choosing stencils, make sure they are continuous line or machine-quilting stencils. Hand-quilting stencils have too many starts and stops and will be frustrating.

Rulers

If you are quilting on a longarm quilting machine, make sure you have a good-quality ruler. I use a 2″ × 12″ acrylic ruler. It is great for marking lines and for guiding the machine along straight lines and seams.

Notions

Don't forget the little things such as pins, scissors, and extra needles.

Additional Supplies for Domestic Sewing Machines

Quilting Gloves

These gloves by Machingers are awesome! They help you grip your quilt and maneuver it through your domestic sewing machine (DSM). This will help you focus more on your quilting and less on wrestling with the quilt.

tip

Quilting gloves are great for longarm quilters, too. They allow you to hold on to your rulers and templates securely without cramping your hands.

Supreme Sliders

One of the biggest complaints of quilting on a DSM is the drag of the quilt on the machine. Pushing and tugging your quilt can leave you worn out and ready to call it quits. The Supreme Slider is a Teflon sheet that lies on the bed of the sewing machine and allows the quilt to slide through the machine with less friction. Most machine quilters wouldn't consider quilting without one of these handy tools.

Free-Motion Foot

When machine quilting with your DSM, you will need a presser foot made especially for free-motion machine quilting. This type of presser foot (sometimes called a darning foot) allows you to see your quilting area and disengage the feed dogs, and it will make your quilting experience even better.

Section 2
THE DESIGNS

In this section, you get to jump in and start learning the designs. Each chapter features designs based on shapes: Swirls & Circles, Squares, Lines & Vines, and Arcs & Points. Each chapter will start with simple, basic designs and progress to modern variations of those designs.

At this point, if you are new to machine quilting, learning the designs may seem overwhelming. It may sound crazy, but think of quilting as handwriting. First, you start learning the design just as you learned your letters, drawing them over and over (and over and over) again until you are comfortable with them. When you feel confident, move to your machine and start practicing them. Then, just as you developed your own handwriting, your quilting will take on a flair of its own, and soon it will be as natural as signing your name.

tip

One of my favorite tools for practicing free-motion quilting designs is a Magna Doodle. Yep, those handy magnetic drawing boards that magically erase are fun to draw on and don't waste paper.

The quilting designs in this section are ones I find myself often using when quilting modern quilts. Some may not look "modern" at first glance, but the texture they add to any quilt is outstanding.

The only thing you need to remember is that with practice, anyone can do these designs.

Are you ready? Let's get to it!

SWIRLS & CIRCLES

When most quilters start free-motion quilting, the swirl and circle shapes are usually the first designs they learn. There is something soothing, almost meditative, when it comes to quilting swirls. Plus, no one can deny that the look they add to a quilt top is the best!

Swirls are a great place to start because they don't have to be perfectly even. The trick to making these look even is to keep the spacing consistent. Also, making the designs smaller or larger can drastically change the look. These designs work well on almost any kind of quilt, and they play well with other designs.

Most modern quilts are filled with geometric shapes and lots of negative space, so circular free-motion quilting designs fit right in. Try quilting them densely to add texture, or leave them open and free to fill in large areas.

Close-up of **CIRCLES** (page 97)

Basic Swirl

This design is very simple, and all the other swirl designs are based on this shape. The basic swirl is great for filling large areas as an allover design. The trickiest part of quilting basic swirls is not getting yourself caught in a corner. Just keep practicing and soon you will be swirling all around.

 1. Start from the edge of the quilting area and quilt a curvy line that curls in on itself.

2. Immediately change directions and echo the swirl until you are back to the edge of the quilting area.

Note: The biggest problem new quilters have with this design is they don't finish the second half of the swirl. Make sure you return to the bottom of the swirl before starting the next one.

After you have quilted the first swirl, you have a choice to make: Depending on where you want to go, you can either echo the first swirl or start a new swirl. In these instructions, I quilted another swirl.

3. From the ending point of the first swirl, quilt the inside of another swirl.

4. Then, echo the outside of the second swirl, just as you did the first, until you reach the edge of the first swirl. It doesn't have to touch, but get it close.

5. Echo the swirl again to move to the other side of the swirl.

6. Quilt another swirl.

7. Continue quilting swirls and echoing until you fill the whole area.

Swirled Hook

What makes this design different from Basic Swirl is that we add a small hook. This design is great for more masculine quilts and is helpful when you need a swirl design that can fit into tight spots, such as the points of triangles.

1. Starting from the edge of the quilting area, quilt the inside of a basic swirl.

2. Immediately quilt a gentle, curvy line extending out from the center. This "hook" doesn't have to point anywhere in particular; just try to fill in the empty areas evenly.

3. Echo the curved line until you are approximately ¼" from touching the edge of the inner swirl.

4. From that point, echo the swirl until you reach the beginning of the swirl.

5. You can echo the swirled hook, or immediately quilt another one. Continue until you finish filling the area.

Paisley

Paisley is another quilting design that is commonly used, but the texture it adds to modern quilts makes it a personal favorite. Paisley might not look like a swirly design, but because the construction is similar, it has been included in this chapter. You can quilt this design larger to use as an allover design or smaller to fill small areas.

1. From the edge of the quilting area, quilt a curved teardrop shape that ends near the beginning point. I like the movement the slightly curved shape gives to the quilting.

2. Echo the shape twice.

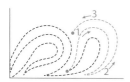

3. Quilt another paisley shape, gently curving it to fit close to the first one.

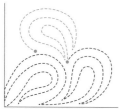

4. Echo the paisley twice, ending close to the first shape.

5. Continue quilting the shapes and echoing until you fill the entire area.

tip

If you find yourself stuck in an area too small for a paisley shape, echo other paisleys until you fill in the area.

Loop & Double Loop Swirls

Even though Loop & Double Loop Swirls are the first step to Pebbles (next up on our list), they are fun on their own. I like to use this design in small sashing or in larger areas to fill in with quilting that is less dense.

This design is a basic meandering line with a loop thrown in randomly.

1. Starting at any edge of the quilting area, quilt a wavy line with a loop at the end.

2. Without stopping after quilting the loop, continue the wavy, meandering line. Add another loop.

3. Continue the design, winding around in random directions, and filling in the entire area.

Instead of single loops, try quilting double loops to add even more detail to the quilting.

1. Start with a wavy line with a loop at the end.

2. Quilt a second loop circling the first one, ending at the same point.

3. Continue quilting the design until the whole area is quilted.

tip

You can quilt double loops in a straight row to fill narrow, straight areas.

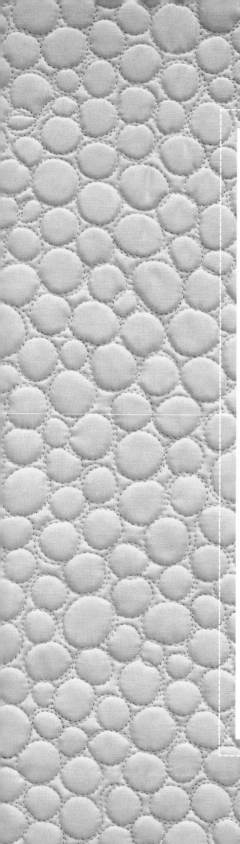

Pebbles

If we vacuum packed the loopy design until all the circles were stuck together, we would have pebbles. Pebbles are easy to quilt but can be very time consuming—although the effort required is worth it. This design adds great texture and can be quilted in varying sizes to give different effects.

1. Start with a circle.

2. Without stopping, quilt another circle that touches the first one.

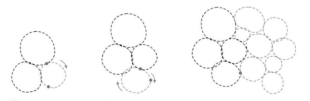

3. Continue quilting circles that touch each other until the whole area is filled.

tip

When quilting the pebbles, trace around some of the pebbles an extra time to add more texture to the design.

Modern Variation

Try quilting the pebbles in various sizes to give a different texture.

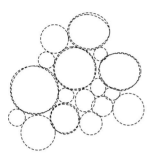

You can quilt ovals instead of circles if you like.

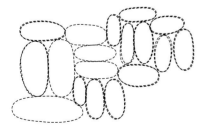

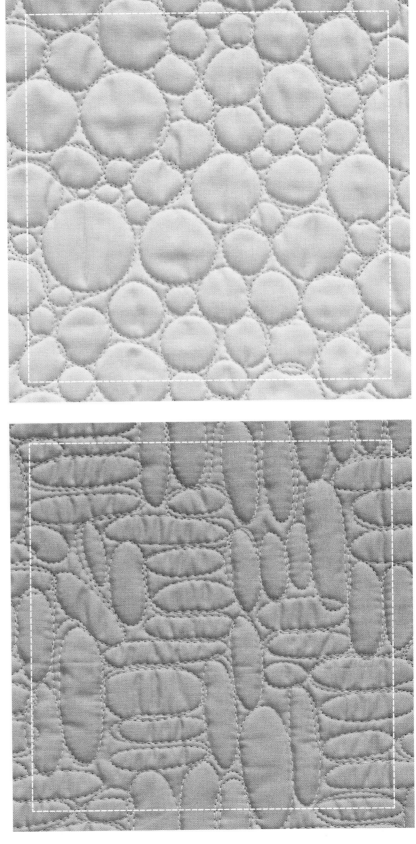

Concentric Circles

Concentric Circles are the more precise cousins of the Basic Swirl. They like their spacing to be even and consistent. Even though they often frown on looser, uneven swirls, they play well with other designs. Try combining them with Paisley (page 24) or Allover Leaves (page 66) or using them to fill in around motifs such as the Plume Feather (page 60) or Faux Rope (page 47).

Using this motif adds a lot of dense quilting. Use in big, open areas of the quilt—the fewer edges to go around, the better.

tip
_____

At all times you want your circles to touch the edge of another circle or the edge of the quilting area. This will help ensure that no areas are left unquilted.

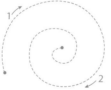

1. Quilt a spiral going inward, trying to keep the distance between the rings about ½".

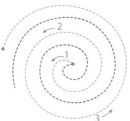

2. When you reach the middle of the spiral, stop and quilt back out of the spiral, keeping the stitching between the lines of the spiral. Continue until you are near the starting point of the circle.

3. Congrats! You have quilted your first circle. To add more circles, travel along the edge of the first circle about 1"–2". Quilt another circle the same as you quilted the first, ending on a line of the first circle.

4. Travel along the edge of the first circle about ¼" and echo the second circle, keeping the spacing about ¼". You should end up on the other side of the second circle, touching the edge of the first circle.

Note: By traveling along the edges of the circles, you will give the illusion that circles float on top of one another. It takes a little more time, but the result is well worth it!

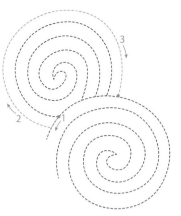

5. Travel along the edge of the first spiral about ¼" and add another ring to your second circle.

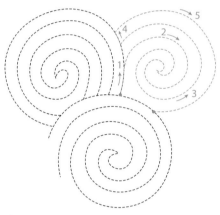

6. When you decide that the second spiral is the size you want, travel ¼" along the outer edge and begin another swirl.

7. Continue until you have filled the quilting area.

Seafoam

Now that you know how to quilt Concentric Circles (page 28) and Pebbles (page 26), you can combine the two to create a whole new design. I named this design Seafoam because the swirls (Concentric Circles) look like ocean waves, and the small circles (Pebbles) look like the bubbles made from the swirling water.

tip

Like the Concentric Circles design, Seafoam is best used in large areas of the quilt. You can use it as an allover design, or to highlight certain areas.

1. From the edge of the quilting area, quilt a Concentric Circle.

2. At the end of the first Concentric Circle, add a few Pebbles. In this illustration, I added 5, but you could add more or fewer, depending on your preference and the area to be filled.

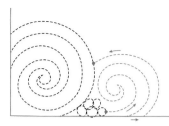

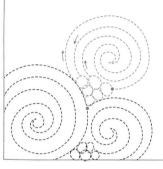

3. After quilting the last Pebble, quilt another Concentric Circle. Echo the outside of the circle until it is the size you want.

4. At the end of the second Concentric Circle, add more Pebbles. Quilt another Concentric Circle.

tip

Use the Pebbles to fill in the spaces between Concentric Circles; these are normally hard to quilt.

5. Continue alternating between Concentric Circles and Pebbles until the quilting area is filled.

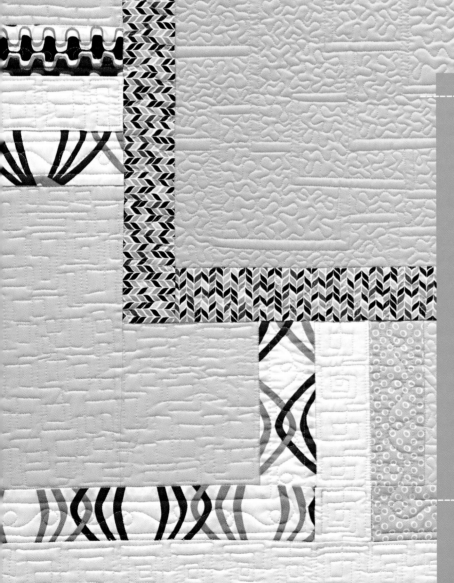

SQUARES

Once relegated to the bottom of the list of go-to designs, square-shaped quilting designs are making a comeback—and in a huge way. Not only are they one of the easiest designs to quilt, but they fit right in with the geometric blocks of modern quilting. All the square-shaped designs in this chapter are great for quilts that have a lot of negative space or geometric blocks. This could include, but is definitely not limited to, Square-in-a-Square quilts, strip quilts, or improvisational pieced quilts. From the background to the sashing, there is no limit on where you can use these designs!

Close-up of **SQUARES** (page 79)

Geometric Allover

This boxy quilting design is great for beginners. You can make the shapes bigger or smaller, depending on how dense you want the quilting to be. Just channel your inner square (or rectangle) and let loose. I am going to show you an example of this design, but it is only to give you an idea of how to quilt it. There is no right or wrong way to make the shapes. Just let the design flow!

1. Starting from the edge of the quilt or a block, quilt a square.

2. Extend the line of the quilting past the square and quilt another square.

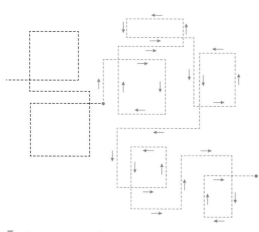

3. Continue quilting squares or rectangles, filling in the whole area.

tip

Have a plan. Working from left to right, or up and down, can help you fill in spaces without getting trapped in a corner.

Chain Squares

Quilting squares in orderly rows can be more calming and less distracting than a Geometric Allover. They are great in sashing and large background areas where you don't want the quilting to be distracting. When quilting this design, you can work horizontally or vertically, making rows of similarly shaped squares to fill the area.

tip

If you would like, you can mark a line on the quilt to help you keep the squares straight.

1. Starting from the edge of the area you want to fill, quilt the outside of a box, leaving a space between the side and the top of the box.

2. Echo the inside of the box approximately ¼" inside the previous stitching, leaving a space at the end. You should end up with a shape that looks like this.

3. From this point, quilt to the right, crossing the lines you just quilted and extending the line approximately ¼" past the square you just quilted.

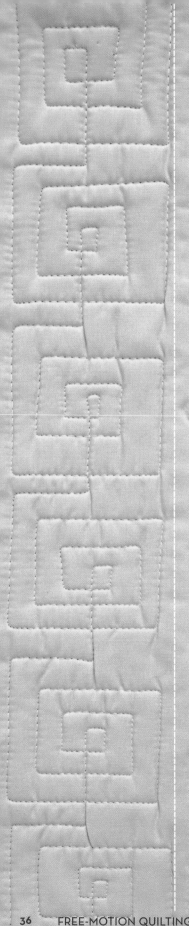

4. Quilt 3 sides of another box, trying to keep the box the same size as the previous box and in line with the first box. Stop at the end of the bottom side, ending ½" from the edge of the first box.

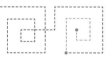

5. Echo the inside of this box ¼" from the outer stitching, just as you did with the first box, ending in the middle of the square.

6. Exit this box the same way you did the first time, extending the line ¼" past the outer edge. Repeat Steps 3–5 until you reach the end of the quilting area.

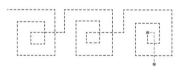

7. When you finish the row, you don't have to tie off and start over. Instead of quilting to the right from the center of the box, quilt down.

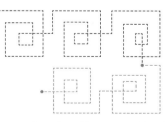

8. Continue making boxes heading the opposite direction until you reach the end of the quilting area. You can quilt several rows without stopping.

Modern Variation

Instead of keeping all the squares the same size, try varying the sizes of the squares to add a different look to the design.

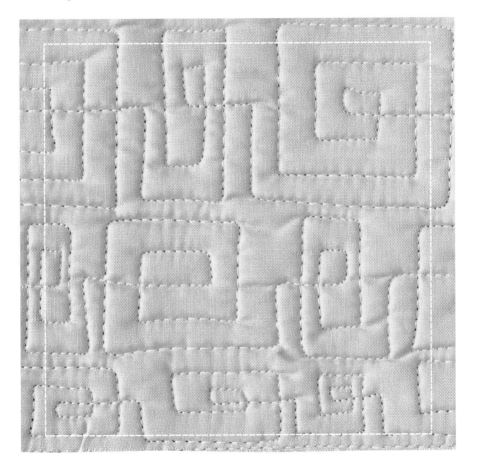

Square Flowers

If flowers were square, this is what they would look like. With a middle square and boxy petals, this design will add interest and depth to your quilt. This design is best used in large backgrounds where it can bloom. Try quilting several square flowers, or add one or two for visual interest.

tip
_____

Start away from the edge of the quilt or block; this design starts in the center and works its way outward.

1. Pick your starting point. Quilt up ½", to the right 1", down 1", to the left 1", and up ½". You are halfway between the top and bottom of the left side. This is the center of the square flower.

2. Now quilt the square petals. Quilt away from the square ½" inch.

3. Quilt up 1" and to the right 1".

4. Quilt a line down to the top edge of the square, and then trace it right back up to the top of the line. This is going to form a "petal" of the flower.

5. Quilt a line 1" to the right, past the edge of the square. Quilt a line 1" down.

6. Quilt a ½" line in to the right edge of the square, and then trace it back out to where you started. You have added the second petal.

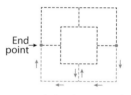

7. Repeat Steps 2–6 around the last 2 sides of the square, ending so that you are touching the first petal. This completes the first layer of petals.

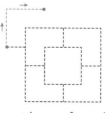

8. Travel along the left side of the petal approximately ½" and then quilt a ½" line to the left.

9. Now you will add the next layer of petals. Quilt up 1" and to the right 1".

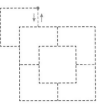

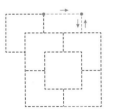

10. Quilt down ½″ to the top of the petal and trace the line back up to the starting point.

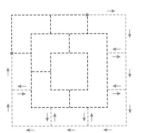

11. Quilt to the right 1″, then down ½″, and trace back up the line to where you started.

12. Continue around the design until you have reached the desired size. When you are done, end with the last quilting line touching the flower to give a completed look. Tie off the thread and repeat with another flower.

Note: If you are not a fan of starting and stopping, make your flowers bigger by starting with a larger center square and making the petals wider. The overall texture of the design is the same, regardless of the size of the individual flowers.

tip

Quilt the petals different sizes or make the corners rounded to add an organic feel to the design.

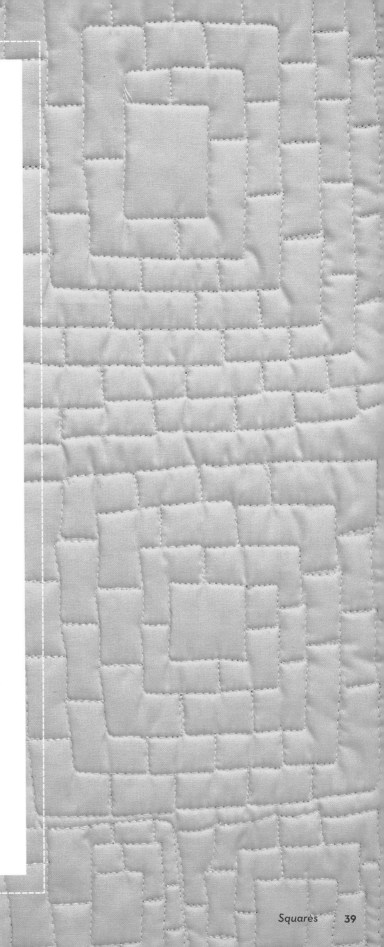

Tiles

When you really want to add dense quilting to your quilt top, Tiles is the design to use. The combination of rigid borders and swirly insides adds so much texture and can really add some fun to large sections of open space. Even though it is an intermediate design, it is not too difficult. The hardest part is deciding where to place the next tile. After a little practice, you will have it down pat!

tip

Try quilting a few tiles randomly among a geometric allover design.

Start and end point →

1. From your starting point, quilt a square the size that you desire. If you want denser quilting, make it smaller. If you want less dense quilting, make it larger. For this illustration, the square is 2″. Stop in a corner of the square.

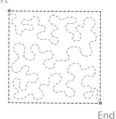

Start

End

2. From this corner, quilt an allover design, filling the square and ending at another corner of the square.

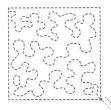

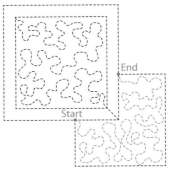

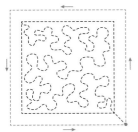

3. From the corner, quilt out diagonally about ¼".

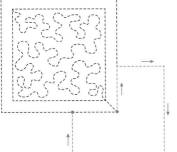

4. Echo the outside of the square. You can space the echo out as close or as far as you would like. I usually space it out ¼". Stop at the starting point of the echo square. This is the first tile.

5. Now you will quilt the next tile. From the ending point, travel along the outer line of the first tile approximately 1". You are going to start the next tile from this point. Quilt to the right 1", making a partial side of the square; quilt 2" down; quilt 2" left; quilt up 1", ending on the side of the first square.

Note: *The great thing about this design is that the tiles look as though they are lying underneath one another, giving the illusion of depth.*

6. Fill in the second square with the allover design, ending at the point where the square touches the first one.

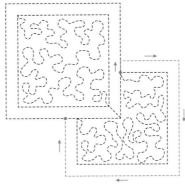

7. Travel ¼" along the edge of the first tile. Echo around the second tile approximately ¼".

8. Repeat again and again, filling in the entire area. Don't be afraid to make the tiles different sizes.

tip

To quilt a modern variation of Tiles, quilt the design with irregular shapes to add a funkier, jagged twist.

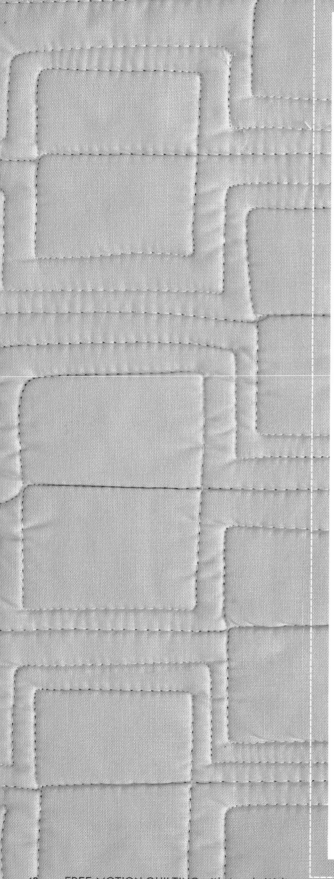

Atomic Squares

This design might look complex, but it is really the same shapes alternated to fit within each other. When quilting this design either horizontally or vertically, you can mark the quilt to keep the lines straight, or you can go for a more organic look by freehanding the lines. This design is great in borders, backgrounds, and blocks with rectangular shapes.

1. Quilt a straight line, approximately 6″ long, from the edge of the area to be quilted.

2. From that point, quilt up 1″, to the left 2″, down 2″, to the right 2″, and up 1″ to form a square approximately 2″ all around.

3. Extend the line 6″ past the square and quilt another square.

4. Continue quilting the squares until you reach the end of the area you are quilting.

5. When you reach the end of the row, quilt down about ¼″.

6. Quilting to the left, echo the squares and lines you just quilted about ¼″ away. Continue until you arrive at the beginning of the row.

7. Now that the first row is finished, quilt a second row that is offset from the one above.

8. Quilt down the side of the section 2½", quilt a line to the right that is approximately 3" long, and quilt your first square for the row.

9. Quilt a 6" line to the right, and then quilt another square that fits in the space between the upper 2 squares.

10. Repeat until the second row is finished. Quilt down ¼" and echo the second row of squares, quilting back to the left.

11. Repeat the alternating rows until you have filled the area with quilting. When you are finished, go back to the top of the quilting area and add an echo to the top of the first row. This will give it a finished look.

12. If you would like the empty spaces at the top and bottom of the design to be filled, add rows of half squares.

13. When finished, there should be no empty areas.

LINES & VINES

These designs were made for traveling. They are generally longer than they are wide and fit well in skinnier places. Use them to fill sashing, borders, or other narrow spaces. You also can use them to break up large areas of negative space.

LINES AND VINES, 35″x 40″, pieced and quilted by Angela Walters

Swirl Scroll

In this design you use the Basic Swirl (page 21), but instead of an allover design, it is quilted in a row. What makes this design handy is that it uses the edges of the block as your guide. This means no marking is necessary, and it can be easily adjusted to fit irregular shapes.

This is an easy design to quilt, but you may have to practice it a couple of times to get the hang of it. You will quilt up one side of the design and back down the other side, returning to where you started.

 1. Start from the bottom of the quilting area approximately ¼" from the edge. The first side of the swirl should extend just past half of the width. Quilt the inside of a Basic Swirl.

 **2.** Echo back out of the swirl, stopping where you start to go down the other side. Try to get within ¼" from the left edge of your quilting area.

 **3.** From this point, sharply change directions and quilt an arc shape about the length of the first swirl. Try to keep it in line with the swirl below it and about ½" from the edge.

4. At the end of the arc, don't stop. Quilt the inside of the next swirl and echo back out until you are almost on the downhill side.

5. Repeat the swirls and arcs until you are near the top of the block. Quilt the inside of another swirl.

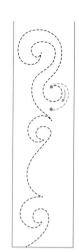

8. Echo out of the swirl, stopping when you are within ¼" of the design.

6. This time, echo the swirl all the way around until you are inside the arc below it.

9. Sharply change direction and echo around the swirl below.

7. From this point, quilt back down the other side of the design, fitting the swirls inside the arcs you quilted earlier. When you are in the middle of an arc, quilt the inside of a swirl. This swirl will face the opposite direction from the swirls you quilted earlier.

10. Continue down the design, alternating between swirls and arcs. You will end at the bottom of the design.

Faux Rope

Faux Rope is a little fancy but could be perfect for the right kind of quilt. This design uses no markings, and it begins and ends in the same place, which makes it efficient as well as striking.

The Faux Rope is quilted in two sections, first the top and then the bottom. Before you start, determine where the top of your design will be. This might be the top of a block or a line you have marked on your quilt top.

Top of quilting area

Bottom of quilting area

1. From the middle of the bottom edge of your quilting area, quilt a gentle S curve, ending in the middle of the top edge.

2. From this point, quilt the same gentle S curve, ending when you are touching the middle of the design. You want this line to be about ¼″ from the right edge.

3. Trace back over the curve you just quilted until you are below the curve.

4. At that point, quilt another gentle S curve that bows out toward the edge of the quilting area and ends at the middle of the top edge.

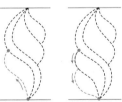

5. Now that you have completed the top portion of the design, echo along the middle of the design, ending at the middle of the bottom edge.

6. Quilt the bottom half of the rope the same as you quilted the top.

If you would like to make your faux rope stand out more, you can quilt Pebbles (page 26) up the center spine.

Figure 8

This design isn't difficult, but getting the rhythm down was always a little tricky for me. Practice it, and you will get it in no time! This design is one of my favorites for long, thin areas, such as borders. When quilting this design you will use the top and the bottom of the quilting area as your guide.

1. From the bottom corner of the quilting area, quilt an S shape that just barely grazes the top edge of the quilting area.

2. Without stopping, quilt a backward S shape. You want it to curve out and come back in and just barely touch the bottom part of the first S.

3. Once you are almost to the bottom edge, quilt another curve out and back to touch the top curve.

This design looks the best when there is no space between the curves, the top or the bottom. This can be a little tricky, but it becomes easier with practice.

4. Continue quilting the alternating curves until you reach the end of the quilting area.

Wavy Lines

Oh, how I love wavy lines! They are one of my all-time favorite designs. You can use them to draw your eyes to a focal point of your quilt or to add movement, whether vertical or horizontal. It seems like every week I am finding more and more uses for this easy, versatile design.

1. For vertical or horizontal wavy lines, determine the top and bottom of your quilting area. Starting at a corner, quilt a gently wavy line to the top.

2. Trace along the top of the quilting area about ¼" and then quilt a wavy line down to the bottom. Do not worry about keeping the lines the same.

3. Trace along the bottom of the quilting area ¼" and then quilt another wavy line up to the top.

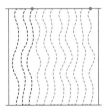

4. Continue until you reach the end of the quilting area.

Sunrays

Wavy lines radiating from the center of the quilt are a modern take on traditional straight-line quilting—without the marking and difficulty of quilting perfectly straight lines. They help draw your attention to the center of the quilt.

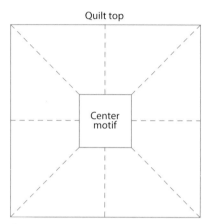

1. Decide on a starting point. I prefer to start on the left and work my way up and around. Mark light registration lines to help you stay on the right angle.

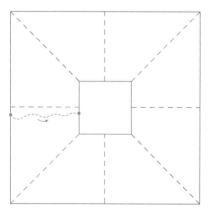

2. Starting from the edge, quilt a wavy line in toward the center of the quilt. Stop at the edge of the center area.

Note: In this illustration, the center of the quilt is a square, but it may be a different shape. The steps are the same; you will just need to take care when tracing along the center.

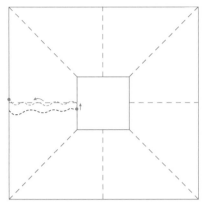

3. Trace up the edge of the quilting area about ¼" and quilt a wavy line to the outer edge of the quilt, ending about ½" above the first wavy line.

Because they radiate from the center, the wavy lines will be closer in the center of the quilt and farther apart on the outer edge. The registration lines you drew will help you keep them even.

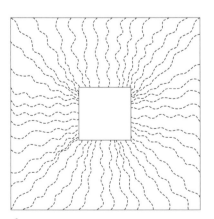

4. Continue quilting wavy lines until you have gone all the way around the quilt.

Modern Variation

Pebbles (page 26) are used with heavy Wavy Lines (page 49) to create a wave.

When quilting wavy lines, quilt pebbles between some of the rays. By making the lines of pebbles random, you will add tons of interest to your quilt.

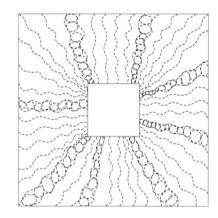

Stacked Triangles

When looking for a funky geometric design, I don't have to look any further than Stacked Triangles. What makes this design a winner is that no marking and no rulers are needed. Simply eyeballing it gives it a more wonky feel and makes the quilting go faster.

1. From the top corner of the quilting area, quilt a line angled down toward the opposite edge of the quilting area. Stop about ¼" from the edge.

2. Quilt a line straight up about 1".

3. From that point, quilt a line angled toward the opposite edge of the quilting area, crossing over the previously quilted line. Stop within ¼" from the edge.

4. Quilt a line straight up about 1".

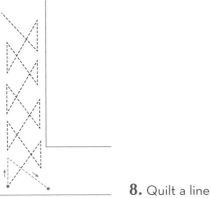

5. Quilt a line angled toward the opposite edge. Try to keep the angle the same as the line above.

8. Quilt a line straight up and then quilt a line that angles toward the bottom edge of the block.

6. Repeat Steps 1–5 until you reach the bottom of the quilting area.

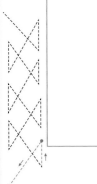
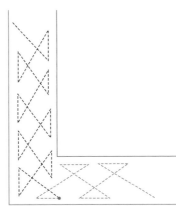

7. If you want this design to turn a corner, end with the line about ¼" from the bottom of the outer corner.

9. Continue the design along the bottom edge the same way you quilted the top.

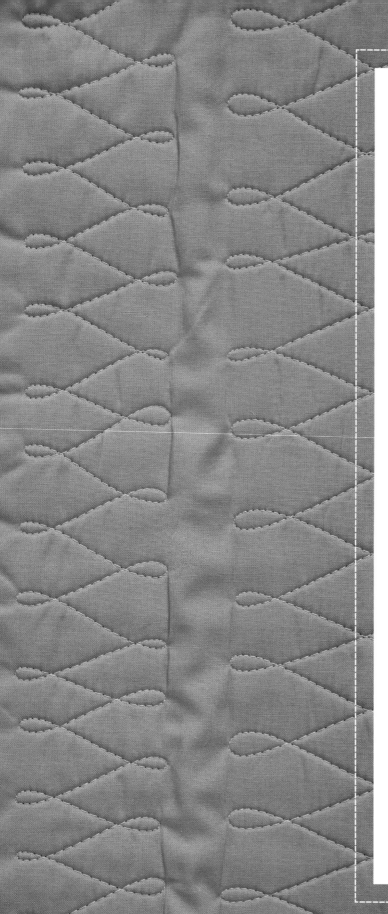

Wishbone

This design is commonly used in machine quilting, but that doesn't mean you should mark it off your list of modern quilting designs. It is so versatile and can fit a wide range of shapes and spaces. Try quilting the wishbones wide and chunky or long and skinny. No matter what you do, you can't go wrong.

 1. From the top corner of your quilting area, quilt a line angled toward the opposite edge. Before you get to the edge, quilt a loop up and around.

 2. Without stopping, quilt another line, angling toward the opposite side.

 **3.** Quilt another loop and head back to the other side.

4. Continue until you reach the end of the row.

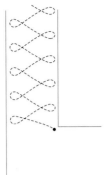

5. If you would like to wrap this design around the corner, end with the line ¼" from the inner point of the corner.

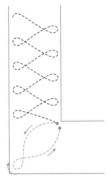

6. Quilt a curving line toward the outer point of the corner. Quilt a loop before you reach the edge, and then curve back toward the inner point.

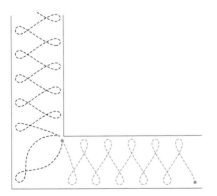

7. Continue along the bottom edge until you reach the end.

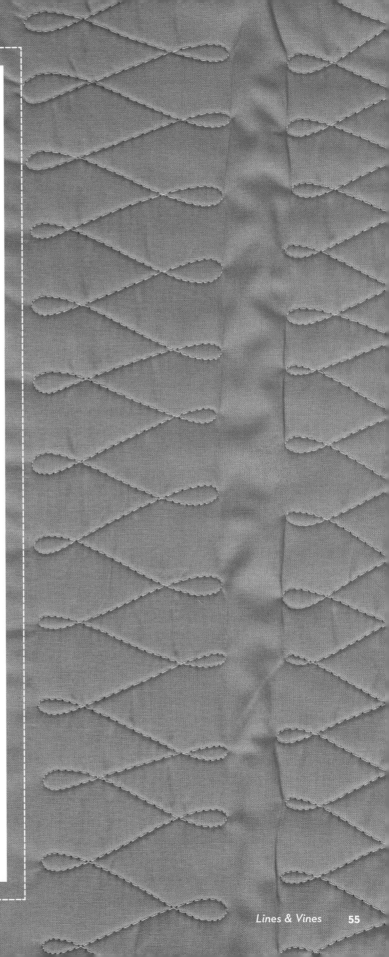

Back & Forth

Probably the easiest quilting design ever, Back & Forth has a stunning impact on any quilt. Use it in wide or skinny areas, long or short areas—any areas! The trick to making this look great is keeping the spacing the same.

1. Starting from the edge of the area to be quilted, quilt toward the other side. Quilt a U-turn right before you touch the edge, and head back to the first side.

2. Before you reach the left edge, quilt another U-turn, and head back to the opposite edge.

Note: *This design looks best when the U-turns don't touch the edges. Try to keep them about ⅛" away from the edges.*

3. Continue to the end of the quilting area.

4. If you want to wrap the design around a corner, stop when the line is near the inner point of the corner.

5. Quilt an elongated loop at a slight angle toward the outer edge. Return to the inner corner.

6. Quilt a second elongated loop that lines up with the outer point. Return to the inner corner.

7. Quilt a third loop that is angled toward the bottom edge of the block. Return to the inner corner.

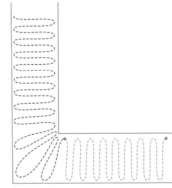

8. Continue quilting the back and forth lines along the bottom of the area.

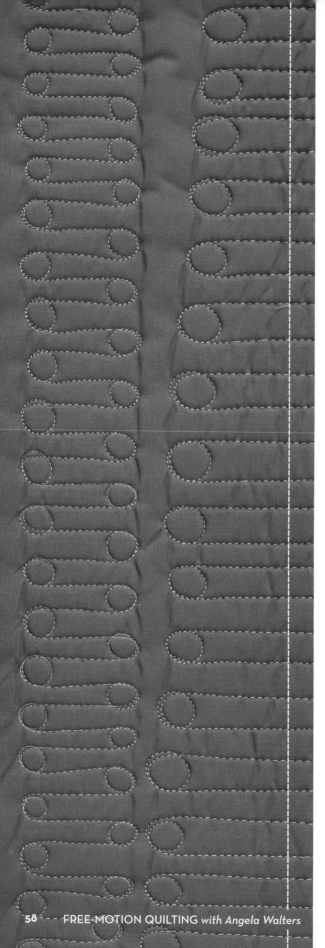

Pulleys

Pulleys is a variation of Back & Forth (page 56). Adding a circle to the design really changes the look of this pattern. It works best in long, skinny areas of quilting.

1. From an edge of the quilting area, quilt a horizontal line toward the opposite edge.

2. As you reach the opposite edge, quilt a small circle. Trace around the circle so you end at the bottom of the circle.

3. Quilt a horizontal line back toward the first edge of the quilting area.

4. Quilt a circle in the same way you did in Step 2, ending at the bottom of the circle.

5. Continue, keeping the spacing consistent, until you reach the end of the quilting area.

Wonky Diamonds

This wouldn't be a modern quilting book if it didn't have any wonky quilting designs! Wonky diamonds are irregular and random, or *organic* to sound fancier. When used in the right quilt, they are a fun diversion from a more structured design.

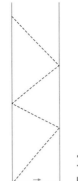

1. From the corner, quilt a line diagonally until it touches the opposite side.

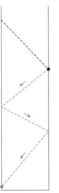

2. Quilt another diagonal line back toward the first side, stopping when you reach the edge. Continue down the area, bouncing from side to side until you reach the bottom.

tip

Don't worry about keeping the lines the same length or angle. You want them to be random.

3. Stop when you reach the bottom corner; then quilt along the bottom until you reach the opposite corner.

4. Quilt back up the quilt, filling in the other side of the diamonds.

5. From the bottom corner, quilt a diagonal line up to the opposite side. Stop when you reach the opposite edge. Try to stop when the point is parallel with the opposite point.

6. Continue quilting diagonal lines until you get to the top of the quilting area.

Plume Feather

The Plume Feather is more of a fern, but whatever you call it, it packs a punch! This design can fill irregular shapes of any height or width and is one of my favorite designs. It can fit in any shape or block, but for this illustration, we will be using a triangle.

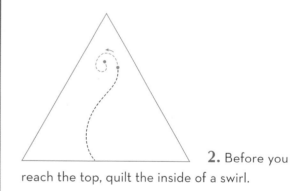

1. From the middle of the bottom edge, quilt a gently curving line toward the top.

2. Before you reach the top, quilt the inside of a swirl.

3. Echo out of the swirl, heading toward the top of the quilting area.

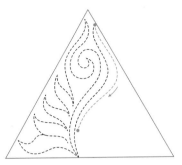

4. Echo the left side of the line, curving around the outside of the swirl and ending when you are touching the center line.

6. Echo back down toward the center line, touching it at the same angle as the line above.

9. Echo the line you just quilted, curving out and back until you touch the center stem. Don't forget to come in at the same angle as the center line.

Note: As you approach the center line, angle down as if you were going to trace the center line. This will make the rest of your design fit better.

7. This is an individual leaf of the feather. Continue quilting the leaves, filling the space until you reach the bottom. End at the starting point.

5. Echo the curve back toward the top, following the same curve. Stop when you reach the edge.

10. Quilt a leaf, echoing out and back to the center line.

8. Echo the main stem until you are ¼″ from the top of the quilting area.

11. Continue quilting the leaves down the side of the design until you reach the bottom.

ARCS & POINTS

When you need something a little curvy or pointy, these are the designs to turn to. The texture that they add to a quilt can really change the way it looks! As with all the designs, practice is key.

Close-up of **ARCS & POINTS** (page 91)

Arcs

This design is so easy that it can be underrated. But don't let the simplicity fool you. Arcs are one of my all-time favorite designs for thinner pieces on a quilt. Wedges, irregular strips, and borders are great places to quilt arcs.

tip

Don't worry about measuring. Once you get in a rhythm, it will be easier to keep the spacing even.

 1. Starting at the bottom, quilt a gentle arc from one side to the other. Try to line up the points parallel to each other.

 2. Travel up the side ¼″ and quilt an arc going back to the other side.

 **3.** Repeat, quilting arcs until you reach the top of the area.

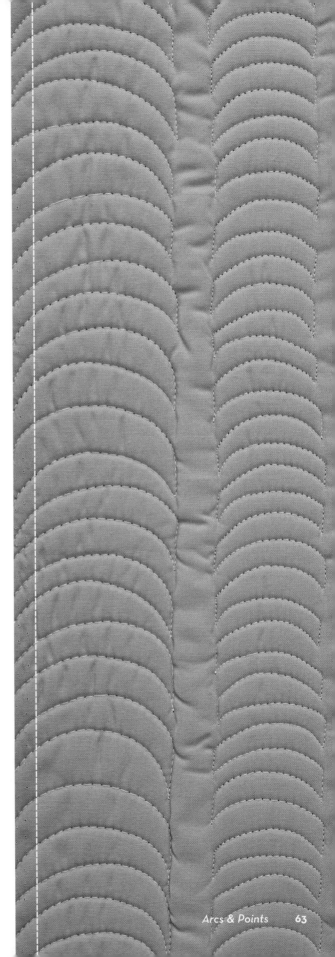

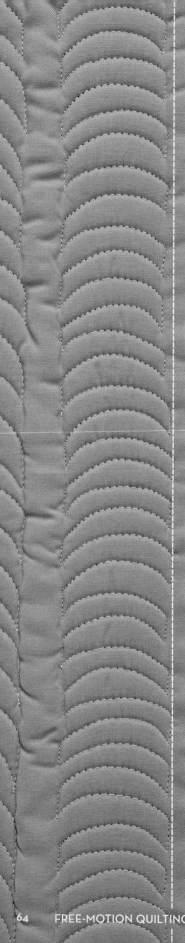

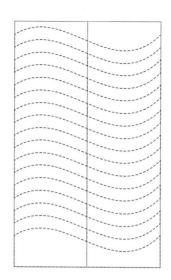

When you have 2 strips next to each other, you can quilt the second one with the arcs facing the opposite way. This gives the illusion of wavy lines.

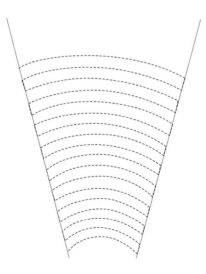

Quilting arcs in irregular shapes is just as easy if you use the sides of the block as your guide.

Modern Variation

You could quilt brackets instead of arcs to add a modern twist to your quilt. Quilt these in the same way; just use a bracket (}) shape instead of an arc.

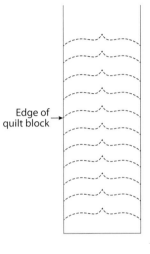

Edge of quilt block

To use the brackets in a different way, try quilting the brackets from corner to corner in a quilt block.

Start and end point

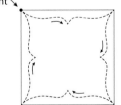

Allover Leaves

This design has been around the machine quilting scene for quite a while, but it can still perform. The Allover Leaves design looks great on a masculine quilt and works best in open areas or as an allover design.

1. From the edge of the quilting area, quilt an arc and mirror it back close to the starting point, forming a leaf.

2. Echo around the point, following the same curve and arriving near the starting point. This is the individual shape that makes up this design. You will repeat this shape over and over until the whole area is filled.

3. From the ending point, curve out in a different direction and back.

4. Echo around the last point and stop when you are near the edge of the first leaf you quilted.

5. Quilt another leaf pointing up and echo it, ending when you are very close to a previously quilted line. You can echo around the leaves several times to move around the quilting area.

6. Continue quilting leaves and echoing them until the whole area is quilted.

tip

You also can make the leaves different sizes so that you are able to fill in the whole area.

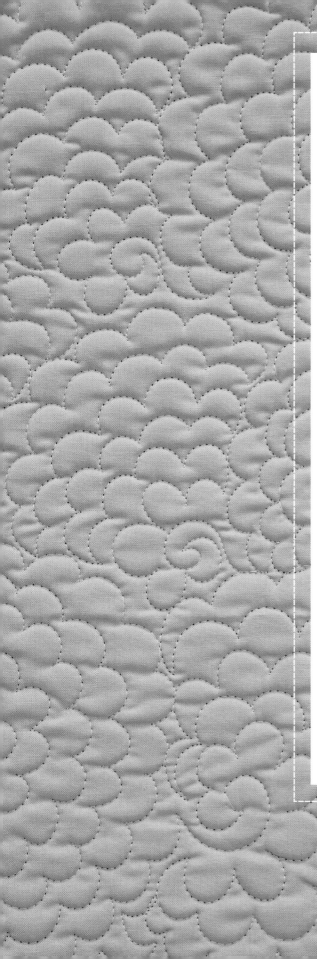

Flower Power

Small arcs quilted around a swirl, Flower Power will definitely add a punch to your quilts. This design is great when used in a row or in the middle of a square block. But like real flowers, they look best in a bunch.

1. From the edge, quilt a small swirl.

2. Once inside the swirl, quilt your way back out of the swirl, making small arcs that touch or come close to the swirl. These are the petals of your flower. Quilt all the way around the swirl.

3. When you reach your starting point, reverse direction and quilt arcs in another layer around the first row. Stop when you make it all the way around the flower.

4. Continue going around the flower until it is the size you like.

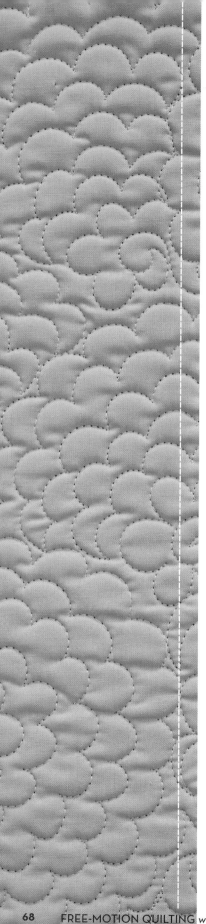

5. When you are happy with the size of the flower, quilt more petals, stopping when you are halfway around the flower.

6. From that point, quilt another swirl extending from the first flower.

7. Quilt petals around the swirl until it is as big as you want.

Note: *When adding the rows of petals to the flowers, you will run into other flowers. When that happens, reverse direction and go back the other way. This will give the illusion that flowers are under each other.*

8. Continue until you have filled the quilting area with flowers.

Variation: Flower Centered in the Block

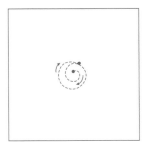

1. Starting in the center of your block, quilt a small swirl. End with the line touching the edge of the swirl. This is the center of your flower.

2. After you have quilted the center, add the petals by quilting small arcs around the center swirl. Stop when you are close to, but not touching, the first arc.

3. Quilt a larger petal that goes up and over the first petal. Have it touch the middle of the first petal. This is where your next row will start.

4. Quilt another row of petals around the flower.

5. Continue until it is the desired size.

You can leave the flower as it is, or fill in around it with a smaller design.

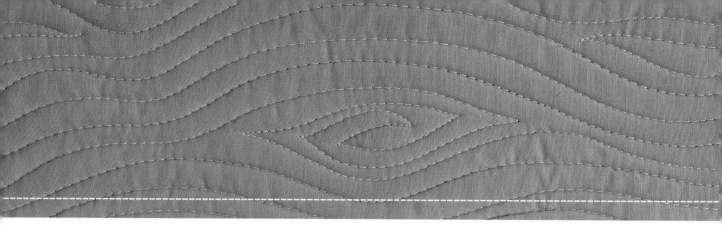

Wood Grain with Knots

When you want tons of quilting and a lot of texture on your quilt, Wood Grain is the design to use. It is quilted from side to side, adding line upon line of quilty goodness. This design works great in large, open areas or as an allover design.

More than with any other design, using a matching thread is key—you want to see texture, not thread.

tip

You can quilt the lines closer together or farther apart, but don't spread them out too much or you will lose the wood grain effect.

KNOT

 1. Start with a gentle arc.

2. Quilt another arc back, stopping ½" from the top and ½" from the side of the first arc.

3. Quilt 2 more arcs going in on themselves, leaving a space of about ½" between the lines. Stop in the middle of the shape. At this point it resembles a swirl with pointed ends.

4. Echo back out, following the curve of the arcs. You will end on the opposite side of your starting point.

WOOD GRAIN

1. Quilt a wavy line from the left side toward the right side.

2. Without stop-

ping, go right into quilting the Knot design shown on page 70.

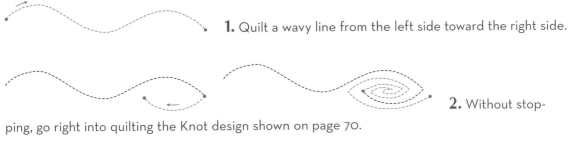

3. Continue quilting a

wavy line, adding random knots. Stop when you reach the edge of the quilting area.

4. Travel up the side of

the quilting area about ¼" and quilt a wavy line echoing back to the left, following the curves of the line below it. Quilt all the way back to the left side.

5. Travel up the left

side ¼" and start quilting toward the right, echoing about ½". As you quilt, add knots in the places where the line below curves down. This makes them look as though they are ingrained in the design.

6. Continue quilting until the wood grain design has filled the whole area.

Mod Clamshell

Clamshell quilting designs have been around almost as long as quilting has. But this classic design gets a modern makeover. Mod Clamshells will add a lot of interest and fun to your quilt, and they are easy to do. The best part: no marking!

tip

Use one row in a narrow sashing, or stack rows on top of one another to fill larger areas. The possibilities are endless!

1. From the beginning of your quilting area, quilt an arc.

 2. At the end of the arc, quilt 2 tiny zigzags. You don't need them to be perfect; you just want a little texture.

3. After you quilt the zigzag, quilt another arc, trying to keep it approximately the same size as the first one.

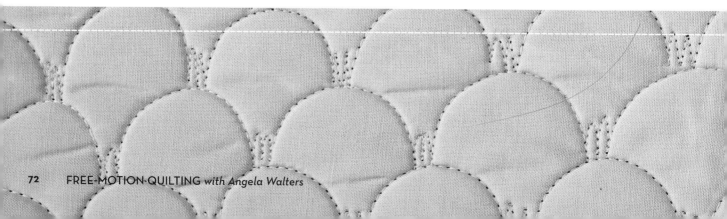

 **4.** Continue quilting until the row is complete.

5. Stacking the rows on top of one another is easy and a great way to fill large areas. After you finish the first row, travel up the edge of the quilting area until you are approximately twice as high as the first row. From the edge of the quilting area, quilt a curved line that touches the middle of the clamshell below it.

6. Quilt 2 tiny zigzags, and then quilt another arc, ending in the middle of the next clamshell. Continue across the row until you reach the beginning of the first row.

7. When you reach the beginning, you should have a row of clamshells with 2 half-clamshells on each side. Continue stacking rows of clamshells until you reach the top of the quilting area.

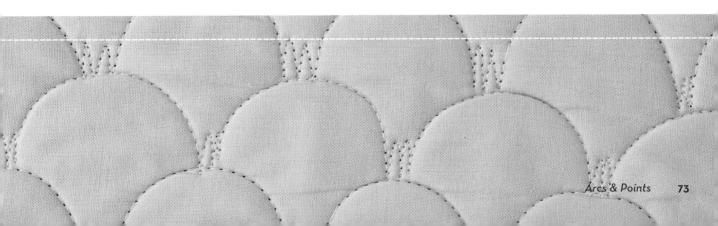

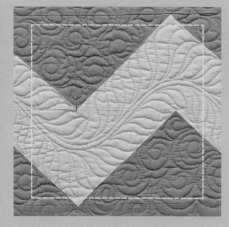

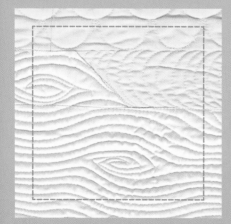

Section 3:
USING THE DESIGNS IN MODERN QUILTS

This is where the rubber meets the road, or more specifically, where the needle meets the fabric. You have practiced your designs several times and are now ready to apply them to your favorite quilts. But in which quilts should you use them, and how? That is exactly what this section is about. I will show you some common scenarios in modern quilts and discuss different options for quilting them.

Disclaimer: The opinions and ideas contained in this section do not necessarily reflect the opinions of the modern quilting community.

I give the above warning in a tongue-in-cheek sort of way, but it is true. Keep in mind that the tips and suggestions I give here are what have worked for me. Take what you like, leave what you don't, and just have fun with the process!

When I am allowed to decide how to quilt my customers' quilts, I usually rely on my own preferences.

My personal motto is, "Quilt until you have quilted too much—and then quilt some more." I love lots and lots of quilting. Most of the quilts you will see in this section are quilted very densely.

I always want the quilting to complement the piecing, not overpower it—a challenge because of my fondness for dense quilting. To accomplish this, I use matching thread that blends with the quilt top.

SQUARE-IN-A-SQUARE & LOG CABIN QUILTS

If the modern quilting movement had a quilt mascot, it would be the Square-in-a-Square quilt, a close cousin to the Log Cabin. Modern quilters love to make these quilts in all shapes and sizes. They can pose a bit of a challenge when choosing quilting designs for them. Depending on the block size, you could be dealing with very wide or narrow pieces, or a combination of both.

Close-up of **FRAMED** (25" × 25", pattern design by Jessica Toye; quilted by Angela Walters)

Close-up of **FRAMED** using different design in center block

When getting ready to quilt Square-in-a-Square quilts, consider a few tips:

- **Highlight just one part of the blocks.**

Even if you want to quilt an allover design on your quilt top, consider doing something different in one area of the blocks. For instance, most Square-in-a-Square blocks have a center square, so consider quilting a different design in the middle. This is one of my favorite things to do.

- **Pick two different designs and alternate between them.**

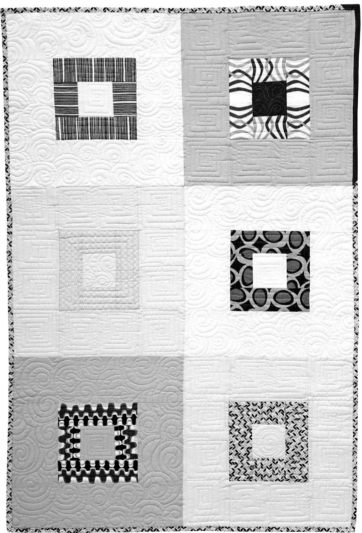

DAISY'S SQUARES, 30" × 44", pieced by Jane Bromberg; quilted by Angela Walters

Deciding on two different designs and using only those will help make the quilting decisions easier.

Close-up of **DAISY'S SQUARES**. The quilting design for each block alternates between Chain Squares and Concentric Circles.

Daisy's Squares is a great example of using only two quilting designs: Chain Squares (page 35) and Concentric Circles (page 28). I alternated them from block to block. This doesn't take much longer than doing one design but adds a much more custom look to the quilting.

tip

To keep the quilting from overwhelming your quilt top, use matching thread, especially when using a number of different designs.

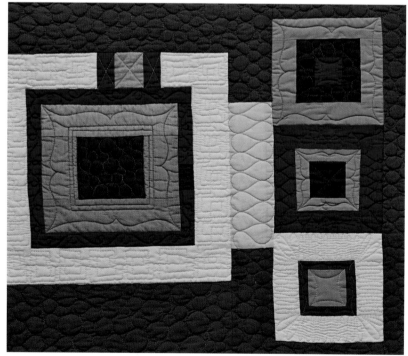

Close-up of **ALL MINE** (page 96)

SQUARES, 34" × 34", pieced and quilted by Angela Walters. Each block is quilted using a different design.

■ Go crazy with it!

Custom quilting is the hardest yet most rewarding way to quilt this kind of quilt. It takes longer, but your effort will be well worth it. Choose several of your favorite designs, and quilt each portion of the block individually.

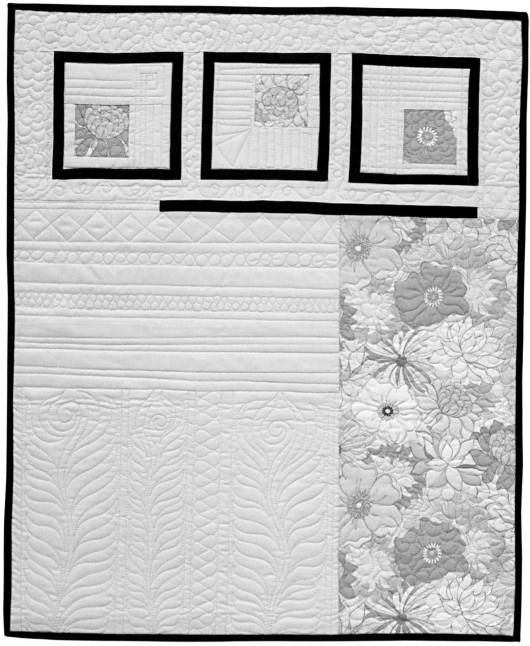

FLOWERS AND CHOCOLATE, 23″ × 29″, designed and pieced by Jenifer Dick; quilted by Angela Walters

■ **Use straight lines.**

Even though this book is about free-motion quilting, straight-line quilting definitely holds a special place in my heart. Combining straight lines with more intricate designs adds interest and a touch of drama. Try quilting a variety of designs using straight lines.

In *Flowers and Chocolate*, I quilted each of the three small blocks a little differently, making up the design as I went along.

ZIGZAG QUILTS

Zigzag quilts have had a surge in popularity in the modern quilting world. Easy and fun to make, they show off fun fabrics and bright solids. However, deciding what designs to use on them can leave you zigzagged out. Consider these options.

Close-up of **FIELD STUDY** (45″ × 57″, quilt pattern designed by Tula Pink; pieced by Georgieanna Martin; quilted by Angela Walters)

ZIGZAGGED, 39" × 47", designed and pieced by Empty Bobbin Sewing Studios; quilted by Angela Walters

Take It a Step Further

Some quilters love to use straight lines that follow the shape of the quilt. But you can take it a step further and add more quilting, making those zigzags stand out.

Try echoing the zigzag, and then filling in the space between with different designs.

Close-up of **ZIGZAGGED** shows the zigzag with straight lines.

Close-up of **ZIGZAGGED**. After you have quilted the lines, you can fill the area with a different quilting design. This example uses Back & Forth (page 56).

Up and Down or Side to Side?

Even though the majority of zigzag quilts have horizontal zigzags, you are not limited to using only horizontal designs. A number of horizontal and vertical designs work well in these kinds of quilts.

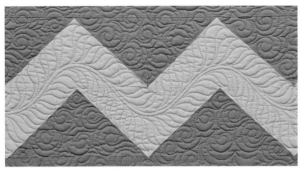

Close-up of **ZIGZAGGED**. A Plume Feather (page 60) is a great example of using a horizontal design when quilting zigzag quilts.

Quilting the Plume Feather on Zigzagged is an example of using a horizontal design. It fills the whole quilting area and helps move your eye across the quilt.

You can also try vertical designs within the zigzags.

Close-up of **ZIGZAGGED**. Quilting vertical designs, such as Pulleys (page 58), is a great way to quilt zigzag quilts.

In this example I used the Pulleys design to quilt the zigzag. Because I used the edges of the quilting area as my guide, I was able to keep the design straight.

Create More Zigzags

If the zigzags in the quilt top tend to blend in, try quilting extra lines to help emphasize the horizontal look of the quilt.

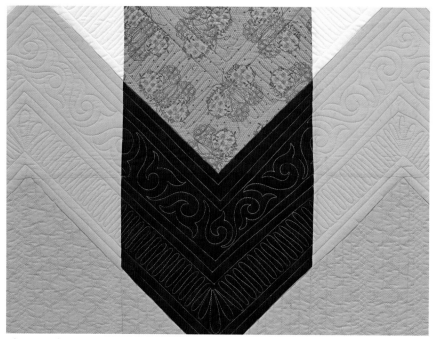

Close-up of **FIELD STUDY** (page 81), showing Swirl Scroll and Figure 8 used in horizontal designs.

For instance, in *Field Study*, I quilted several horizontal lines that followed the piecing. Then I filled in the spaces between the lines with horizontal designs, such as the Swirl Scroll (page 45), Back & Forth (page 56), and the Figure 8 (page 48). Doing this breaks the bigger sections into smaller zigzags, reinforcing the horizontal look of the quilt.

Note: When quilting Zigzagged, I quilted the blue background with an allover design to help provide contrast between the zigzags and the background. However, in Field Study, I quilted the whole area as the foreground, leaving no background. Before quilting zigzag quilts, consider whether you want a background area.

WONKY QUILTS

Wonky quilts—people either love them or hate them. Most people love to make them, but that love quickly cools when it is time to quilt them. All of those irregular shapes can be overwhelming! Instead of being overwhelmed, trying a few simple things can add a custom look to your quilting.

Close-up of **HOUSING PROJECT** (page 87)

Wonky Log Cabins

Oh, wonky Log Cabins...is there anything funkier than that? I think not!

Easy Peasy

Pick one part of a block, such as the outer ring of a block, and quilt a custom design in only that part of the block. Then, quilt the rest with an allover pattern. Doing this will highlight that area of the quilt but will be fairly easy to quilt.

Just a Wee Bit More

If you love the look of custom quilting, you may want to do a little more quilting. Consider quilting the outer ring and center of the Log Cabin block with a custom design and filling in the rest with an allover design.

Close-up of **HOUSING PROJECT**

The quilting in *Housing Project* is a prime example of custom quilting. I quilted the center of the block with Pebbles (page 26) and the outer portion with a Wishbone (page 54) or Back & Forth (page 56).

HOUSING PROJECT, 48" × 53", quilt designed and pieced by Scott Hansen; quilted by Angela Walters

Custom Quilting...or Not?

Under normal circumstances, I hesitate to quilt each part of the wonky Log Cabin block with a separate design. Usually (I say "usually" because there are always exceptions) wonky Log Cabins are bright, funky, and full of different types of fabrics. Quilting each little piece differently can be overwhelming and make the quilt confusing to look at. To keep that from happening, I like to highlight only a few parts of the block and quilt the rest with an allover design.

If you like the idea of custom quilting each of the sections, go for it!

WONKY STARS, 39″ × 49″, pieced and quilted by Angela Walters

Other Wonky Quilts

Of course *wonky* doesn't refer only to Log Cabins; it includes any design that is off-center or askew. When quilting any type of wonky shape, choose designs that use the edges of the quilting area as a guide. The result will be quilting that easily fills the random shapes.

When quilting wonky stars, the points of the stars can be random sizes. A Back & Forth design (page 56) is one of my favorite ways to quilt the random shapes.

For slightly bigger blocks, a small Swirl Scroll (page 45) will easily fit the area, adding a custom look to the quilting.

Close-up of **WONKY STARS**. Using Back & Forth is a great way to add texture to the random shapes of a wonky star.

Close-up of **HOUSING PROJECT** (page 87). The Swirl Scroll design is a great way to fill wonky shapes.

STRIP QUILTS

Strip quilts of all shapes and sizes rank high on the list of fun modern quilts. As fun as they are to piece, they are even more fun to quilt. Because the pieced strips act as a guide, marking your quilt is unnecessary. You can jump right in and start having fun right away.

Close-up of **NEPTUNE** (page 92)

ARCS & POINTS, 53″ × 42″, pieced by Heidi Hendrickson and quilted by Angela Walters

Use All Your Favorite Designs

Try quilting a number of different designs on the quilt, one in each strip. Not only will it add variety, but it also will be great practice.

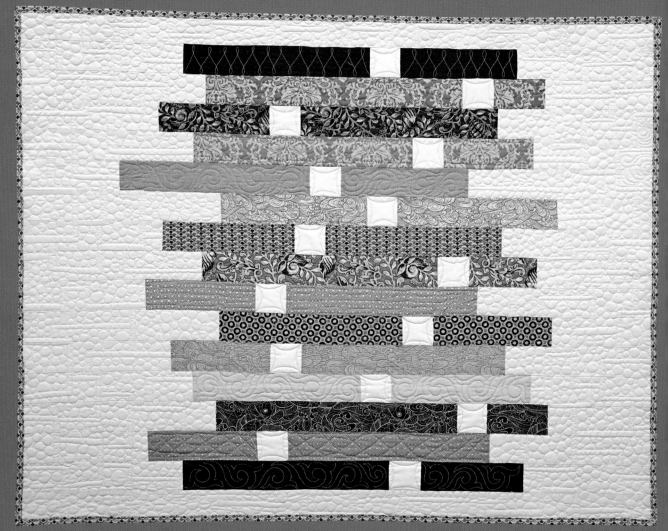

NEPTUNE, 41" × 32", designed and quilted by Angela Walters; pieced by Jane Bromberg.

Almost any of the Lines & Vines designs work well for strip quilts. The designs used in this strip quilt include Swirled Hook (page 23), Stacked Triangles (page 52), and Back & Forth (page 56).

Close-up of **NEPTUNE** shows several designs that work well in strip quilts.

Allover Designs

Allover designs also can work well in strip quilts. Instead of quilting each strip differently, try using allover designs. When quilting *Low Volume*, I picked two quilting designs: Flower Power (page 67) for the white areas and Allover Leaves (page 66) for the rest of the quilt.

LOW VOLUME, 42″ × 55″, designed and pieced by Jacquie Gering; quilted by Angela Walters

Quilting it this way makes the individual strips less noticeable and makes the overall design of the quilt stand out more. Also, using two designs can be quilted as quickly as using one allover design but adds a semicustom look to the quilt.

This may not work in every strip quilt, but it is an option for the right quilt.

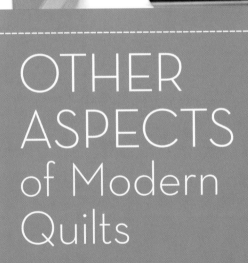

OTHER ASPECTS of Modern Quilts

Modern quilts contain a variety of shapes and designs, so it can be hard to categorize them. However, many modern quilts share certain characteristics. Deciding how to handle these characteristics when quilting can make the difference between good quilting and great quilting.

ALL MINE, 51″ × 59″, pieced and quilted by Angela Walters

Negative Space

Some modern quilters love to add a lot of negative space to create an interesting quilt. But when the time comes to quilt all that space, it can seem like a daunting task. Instead, think of it as your opportunity to run free and let your imagination roam. Nothing makes me happier than seeing a lot of open space on a quilt. Here are some things to consider when quilting negative space.

Blend, Blend, Blend

It can be very easy for the quilting in negative space to distract from the piecing, especially if you use thread that is a different color. Using a matching thread that blends in will ensure that your quilting will add texture but won't overwhelm the piecing.

CIRCLES, 41″ × 55″, **pieced and quilted by Angela Walters**

Mix Up the Quilting Designs

Using the same design in large areas of negative space can make the quilting look boring. To keep it from getting too monotonous, randomly mix in different designs. For instance, if you quilt pebbles on the quilt, add in a couple of swirls to break it up.

Using different designs to break up larger quilting areas will create smaller spaces that will seem more manageable. When quilting *All Mine,* I combined two different designs to make a larger design, breaking up the negative space and adding more detail.

To create the larger design for the lower portion of *All Mine*, I quilted two rows of brackets (page 65) and filled in the space between with Back & Forth (page 56).

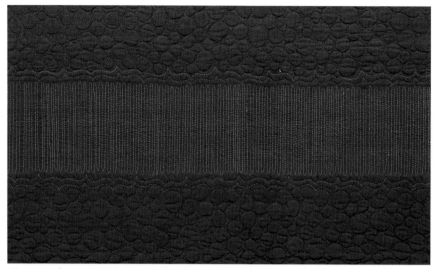

Close-up of **ALL MINE** (page 96). Breaking up the negative space with a larger quilting design will help make the area more manageable.

Quilting the same design in the top portion of the quilt helps to balance the quilting.

Close-up of **ALL MINE**

Almost any design can be used to break up the negative space. You can even use the same design on a bigger scale, as I've done in *Circles* (page 97). You are limited only by your imagination.

Be a Copycat

One of my favorite ways to quilt negative space is to re-create the shapes within the piecing. The quilting echoes the quilt pattern and helps to create unity in the quilt.

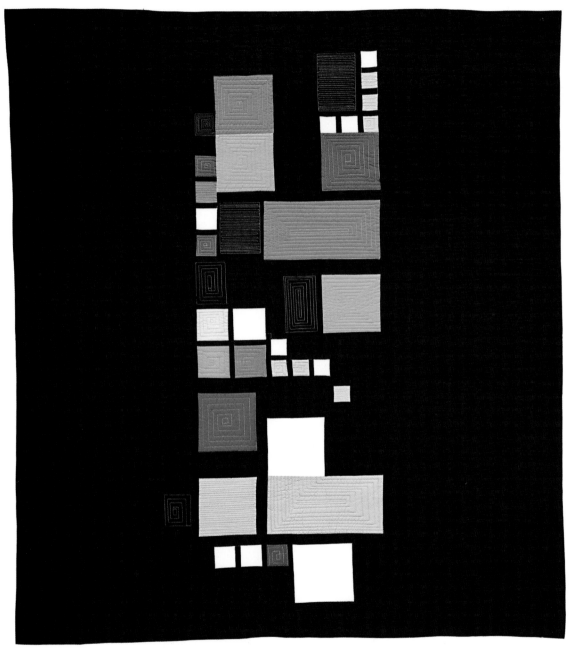

TECHNO, 58" × 51", designed and pieced by Jacquie Gering; quilted by Angela Walters

Note: I broke my own rules when quilting Techno. *I wanted the quilting to look like the piecing, so I quilted a few random blocks in a colored thread. Usually I prefer matching thread in my quilts.*

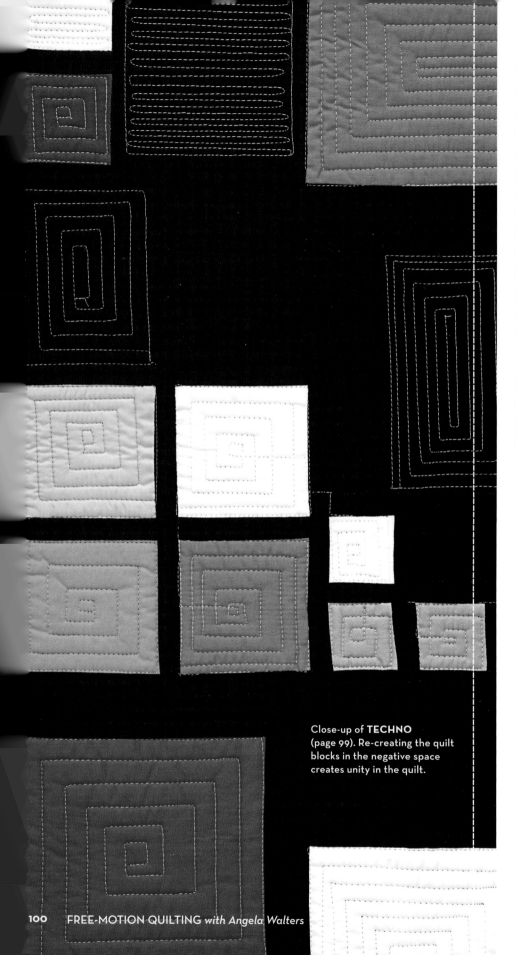

When quilting *Techno*, I wanted to re-create the colored squares with the quilting. I randomly quilted a few squares and rectangles, being careful not to overdo it with the colored thread. When I finished the colored quilting, I filled in the rest of the area with Geometric Allover (page 34) using matching thread.

The great thing is that you can customize the amount of quilting. How much or how little you want to add is up to you.

Close-up of **TECHNO** (page 99). Re-creating the quilt blocks in the negative space creates unity in the quilt.

Extend the Piecing

Sometimes it's possible to extend the piecing into the negative space. This makes the quilting unexpected and a little different. Plus it's just fun to do!

MODERN PLAID, 41″ x 56″, designed and pieced by Alissa Haight Carlton; quilted by Angela Walters

Using the pattern of *Modern Plaid* as my inspiration, I extended the strips into the negative space and quilted it the same as the rest of the block.

Close-up of **MODERN PLAID** (page 101.) Extending the blocks into the negative space is a great way to add a little extra oomph to your quilt.

Extending the piecing into the negative space won't always work. Consider each quilt and evaluate whether you think it will benefit the quilt or detract from the piecing. When used correctly, it is a huge wow factor.

Busy Prints

Bold, bright fabrics are one of the things that jump-started the modern quilting trend. When a quilt has a lot of busy fabrics, it can be tempting to automatically quilt a meander on it. Let me encourage you to try some different things.

Use the Fabric as Inspiration

Chances are, you love the fabric in your quilt. So why not emphasize it? Quilting along the designs within the fabric is quick and easy. And most modern fabrics have a lot of designs to choose from.

BRIOCHE AND BAGUETTE, 37″ × 53″, pattern by Modern Quilt Relish; pieced by Georgieanna Martin; quilted by Angela Walters

The fabric design guides the quilting in **BRIOCHE AND BAGUETTE.**

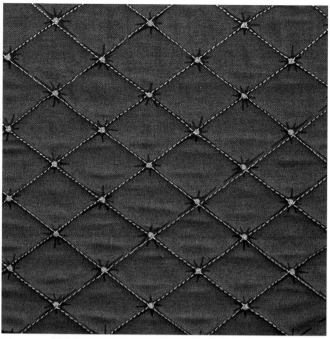

Close-up of **BRIOCHE AND BAGUETTE** (page 103)

Close-up of **BRIOCHE AND BAGUETTE**

Another bonus—no marking!

If you are short on time, quilt around only the elements in the fabric that you like the most. For example, if you happen to love a big flower that is featured, quilt around it and fill in the rest of the area with a different allover design. You can decide how much effort you want to put into it.

The back of the quilt will really show off your hard work.

Close-up of the reverse side of **FLOWERS & CHOCOLATE**

Close-up of **FLOWERS & CHOCOLATE** (page 80). Outlining some of the flowers and filling in the rest of the area with an allover design is a great way to quilt modern fabrics.

Practice Makes Perfect

Because busy prints tend not to show the quilting very well, use those areas as a chance to practice some designs that you aren't completely comfortable with. That way all your bumps and bobbles won't be visible. You can practice worry-free and improve your free-motion quilting. It's a win–win!

Get Funky with It

Quilts made with brighter, bolder fabric can handle quilting that is bolder and funkier as well. So use this as your opportunity to quilt your designs on a bigger scale. Or try using a crazy, funky design you normally wouldn't try. The main thing is to *have fun with it!*

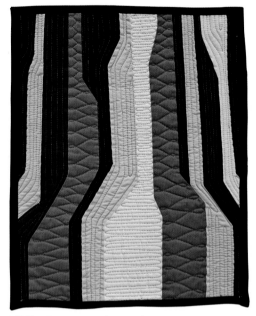

Irregular Shapes

If you are looking at a quilt with a lot of irregular shapes, you are probably looking at a modern quilt. Trying to come up with quilting ideas for those irregular spaces can be difficult, but don't let that discourage you from custom quilting.

Choose designs that use the edges of the blocks as a guide, such as Wishbones (page 54) or Back & Forth (page 56).

By using the pieced edges as your guide, your designs will automatically fit the irregular shapes without marking.

MINI-ME, 13″ × 17″, **designed and pieced by Angela Walters**

SHATTERED GLASS, designed and pieced by Tula Pink; quilted by Angela Walters

Sometimes a simple design is the best way to go. But before you quilt, make sure the design looks good in a range of different sizes.

Close-up of **SHATTERED GLASS**

A simple arc uses the points of the block to make a design that can easily fit any size. This particular design, just a series of arcs, is fast and easy to quilt.

1. Starting at one corner of the block, quilt an arc ending at the 90° corner of the triangle.

2. Quilt another line that gently arcs out, ending approximately at the halfway point of the longest edge of the triangle.

tip _____

Aim for the halfway point—no need to mark the exact center.

3. Quilt another line that arcs the opposite way ending at the same 90° corner.

4. Quilt the last arc ending on the opposite side you started from.

Note: This particular technique is called continuous curve and has been around the longarm quilting community for a while. It is a fast way of quilting custom designs using the points of the block as reference points, and it happens to be one of my favorite techniques!

STILL STUCK?

Tips for Deciding on Quilting Designs

We have all been there—stuck staring at a quilt with no clue how to quilt it. Here are a few final tips to help get you going.

■ **Determine whether there is a "background" to the quilt.**

If you are quilting a busy quilt with a lot of pieces, it might help to determine whether there is a background that you can quilt with the same design. If so, you will only need to figure out how you want to quilt the shapes in the foreground.

When quilting *Mod Bars*, the first thing I did was find the background of the quilt.

MOD BARS, 60" × 75", designed and pieced by Alissa Haight Carlton; quilted by Angela Walters

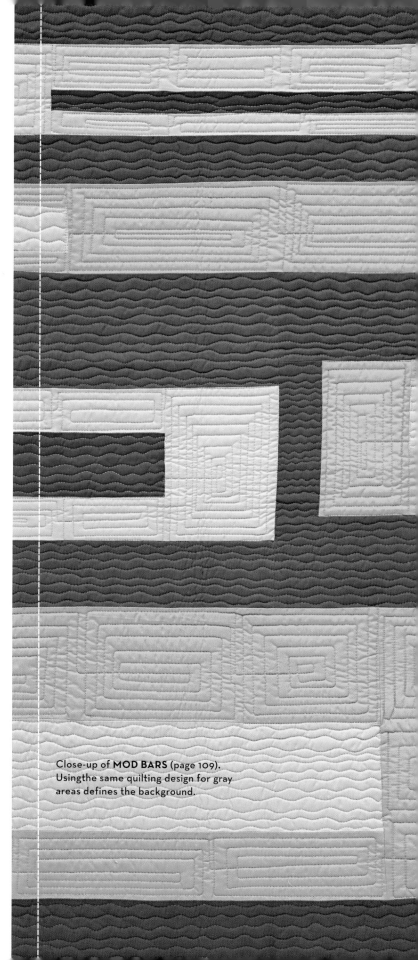

After I determined that the gray fabric would be the background, I quilted the same design on all of the gray pieces. Quilting the background of the quilt in the same way helped to emphasize the rest of the piecing.

A quilt might not have a background, but when it does, use it to your advantage.

Close-up of **MOD BARS** (page 109). Using the same quilting design for gray areas defines the background.

- Ask yourself, "What is the most important thing about this quilt?"

The most important thing about your quilt could be the fabric, the pattern, the piecing, or the fact that it is for a special little boy who will drag it through the mud countless times. When you have established what's most important, you can use the quilting to highlight it.

If the most important thing is the fabric, custom quilt the blocks to feature the fabric. When you want people to notice the quilt pattern first, emphasize the shapes of the pattern. If you know it will get lots of love and washing, quilt it more densely.

When you are able to verbalize the main point of the quilt, choosing a design may be easier.

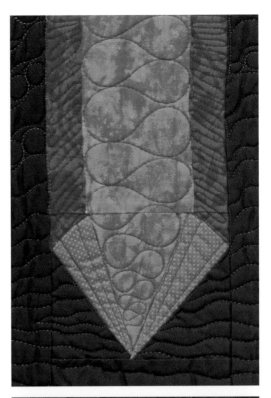

Close-up of **LINES & VINES** (page 44). Wavy Lines (page 49) are used as the background design to set off bold shapes.

■ **Determine the style of quilting you want.**

Think about your favorite quilting designs. Do you prefer swirly, flowery designs? Or are geometric designs your favorite? Deciding on a style of quilting will narrow down the number of designs to choose from.

■ **Start with something.**

Sometimes, you have to start quilting to get your creative juices flowing. If you know how you are going to quilt some of it, go ahead and get started. More often than not, inspiration will strike. Many times I have started quilting a certain design only to change my mind.

■ **Look to the quilt for inspiration.**

All the inspiration you can ever need is right in front of you. Look at the fabric and the pattern for ideas. You may see a floral design you can use, or perhaps you can quilt shapes that look like the blocks in the quilt. The best quilting complements the quilt top. Taking your quilting designs from the quilt top will definitely complement the quilt.

■ **Sleep on it.**

The brain works in mysterious ways. Have you ever had a thought pop in your head at a random time? Quilting inspiration works the same way; so if you can't decide how to quilt it, just take a break. At the very least, it will justify starting a new project!

■ **Change the scale.**

You may love a certain design, but you aren't sure it would look good in your quilt. Try quilting it smaller (or larger) than you normally would. You also can try using different sizes of the same design within the quilt.

When quilting *Brother's and Sister's,* I quilted the same design in different sizes.

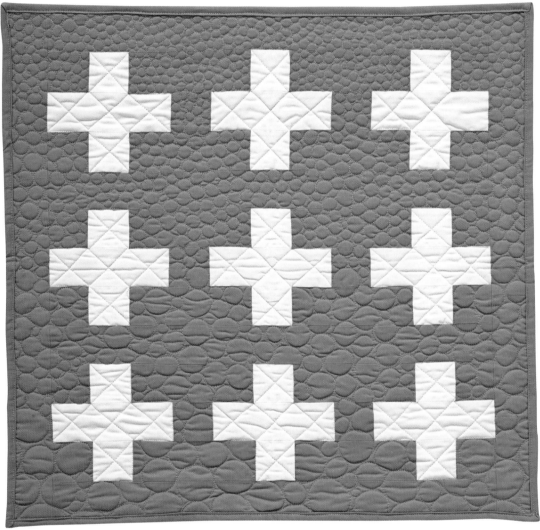

Same design with varying scale used in **BROTHER'S AND SISTER'S,** 25″ × 25″. Designed and pieced by Heather Jones; quilted by Angela Walters.

I quilted the pebbles smaller at the top and larger at the bottom. This is a great way to jazz up the background of a quilt, and it can add a lot of texture as well.

Note: Before I started quilting, I marked lines separating the quilt into several sections. Then I quilted a different size in each section. By gradually increasing the size in each section, the different sizes appear to blend into each other.

■ **Combine designs.**

If you can't decide between two designs, try combining them. It may take a little more thought, but chances are you will end up with something that works out perfectly for your quilt.

Swirl Scroll (page 45) combined with Back & Forth (page 56)

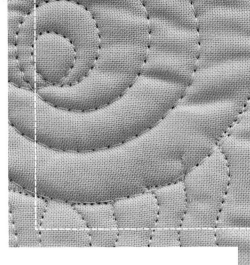

tip

When combining Concentric Circles (page 28) and Wavy Lines (page 49), I first quilted the circles individually and then filled in the empty spaces with wavy lines.

Concentric Circles and Wavy Lines combine to make a completely different design.

Concentric Circles (page 28) combined with Allover Leaves

A swirly design can combine with almost any other design, including Allover Leaves (page 66).

If you aren't sure whether a design will work, try drawing it. That usually will give you the answer.

■ **Use designs in different ways.**

Don't let yourself get stuck thinking that a design can be used only in a certain way. For example, designs that you may consider only for allovers can easily be used to fill borders and sashing.

A perfect illustration of this is the quilting on *Framed* (page 76). Even though it is a Square-in-a-Square quilt, I quilted each area of the blocks with designs that are normally considered allover designs.

I quilted the individual paisleys in a row instead of as an allover design. If you are in love with a design but aren't sure it will fit in the area where you need it, tweak it and play with it until it works.

I hope that by now your head is spinning with some new ideas and that you are motivated to move beyond meandering and into custom quilting.

But if you take only one thing from this book, remember this: Just do it!

Just like anything else, it takes practice, and you can't get better if you never start. Keep trying, keep going, and soon it will be as natural as signing your name.

So here's to you and your new fabulous machine quilting!

Close-up of **FRAMED.** Use designs that are normally thought of as allover designs to fill narrow areas.

GLOSSARY

Allover quilting: The same quilting design across the surface of the quilt

Background: The part of the quilt top that isn't the focus

Custom quilting: Machine quilting different designs in each area of the quilt

DSM: Domestic sewing machine

Echoing: Repeating a previously quilted design a set distance apart

Foreground: The part of the quilt top that is the focus of the quilt, usually the blocks

Free-motion quilting: Hand-guided machine quilting, either on a longarm quilting machine or on a domestic sewing machine; often abbreviated FMQ in quilting blogs

Longarm quilting machine: A machine made especially for quilting that consists of a large frame on which the quilt top, batting, and backing are pinned and a large sewing machine that freely moves around the quilt top, quilting the layers together while it moves

Quilting area: The area of the quilt to be quilted—the whole quilt, certain blocks, or any other area

Semicustom quilting: Quilting that combines custom quilting designs to highlight certain areas of the quilt with allover designs that fill in the rest of the quilt

Straight-line quilting: Quilting that uses straight lines as the design

Traveling: Quilting over a previously quilted line in order to move to a different area to continue quilting

Wonky quilts: Quilts that include blocks that are askew